I0059432

Introduction

Process means everything. Selling a business is a "process" and not an "event". This book walks you, the business owner, through the sale process. Armed with this knowledge, you will be able to more effectively make decisions that will aid in the successful sale of your business.

The M&A Law Firm was established in 1982 and is the only law firm in the Country that focuses primarily on representing middle market business sellers. Unique aspects of this process include, preparation of an initial business profile, selection of the right investment banker, preparation of detailed "seller diligence" information, and using bid templates that result in the receipt of enhanced letters of intent that can be compared on an "apples-to-apples" basis. These are just a few of the advantages provided by the M&A Law Firm as part of its management of the entire sale process from start to finish.

All aspects of the business sale process are expertly integrated in order to make sure that each step is carried out in the best manner possible. You become an educated and informed seller. You build trust and respect with buyers through the use of knowledgeable and experienced counsel. That respect translates into the willingness of buyers to engage in a competitive process to make sure your business sells at the highest price.

The M&A Law Firm sets new standards in successful business sales. Owners of middle market companies (sales of $10M to $200M) have relied on the expert advice and guidance of the M&A Law Firm for over 30 years. The following material is designed to arm you with information to help you understand the proper process to use in selling your business to assure a successful closing on your terms and conditions.

Table Of Contents

CHAPTER I
When Is The Right Time To Sell?

The decision to sell a business is often times dictated both by outside forces and by personal circumstances and desires. Generally, business owners decide to sell based on criteria which includes the following:

1.1   Ability to support future lifestyle. First you should make a reasonable estimate of what the business would sell for. You should then sit down with a qualified professional to determine total sources of income derived based on net cash proceeds from the business sale, along with any other income that you may have. If these revenue sources will be sufficient to pay your expenses and allow you to live your desired lifestyle then selling the business is an option. Like any other financial planning for the future, variables such as remaining lifespan, rates of return, assumptions regarding social security and other government benefits and existing obligations will play a major role in this analysis.

1.2   Positive sales and profits.
When valuing a business, owners often talk about sales price in terms of a multiple of the profits of the company. One of the biggest drivers in determining those multiples is whether or not the company has positive sales and profit growth. Investors are not interested in purchasing a company that is going to be flat for the next three to five years. Buyers want to have a reasonable expectation of growth. It is important, therefore, in order to maximize value, that you sell during a time period when the company has both good revenue and profit growth. Many times a state of euphoria will come over entrepreneurs who are in a growth mode. They believe that things will only get better and they wait until that window closes. When things level off or get worse, then they can't sell the company or end up selling for substantially less.

1.3 The need to reach for the next level of capital investment or management expertise. There comes a time when many entrepreneurs reach the end of their capacity in terms of financial resources and/or management capability. The business may in fact be too successful and may have outgrown your ability to (i) fund its growth (or take the risk required); or (ii) to provide the necessary leadership, expertise and direction to continue to grow the company. At this stage, the company presents a great opportunity for a buyer to capitalize on this pent-up potential and buyers will pay a higher price to obtain that potential.

1.4 Emerging technologies may be squeezing your market. If technology is a significant factor in the ongoing success of your business, there may come a time when that technology starts to become obsolete or significant additional resources will be required to develop advancing technologies. This may again be a good time to sell so that you can capitalize on what you have built to date and will be able to allow a new investor or buyer to shoulder the burden of developing new technologies, while at the same time reaping the benefits from those new technologies.

1.5 Product life cycles. Products also have their own life cycle. When that product life cycle is coming to an end, it may be beneficial to sell before the business starts to decline. Even though the company's products themselves may be on the decline, the company will have valuable assets to sell such as its people, equipment, systems, customers, vendors, information, technology and other intangibles. A buyer could easily capitalize on these assets by putting their products into your channels or taking your products and putting them into buyer's markets.

1.6 Desire to move into the next phase of life. There comes a time when business owners decide that they no longer want the burden of: (i) paying off their line of credit, (ii) resolving employee disputes, complaints or lawsuits, (iii) wondering whether or not one or more major customers may take their business elsewhere, and (iv) contemplating how they are going to meet payroll and make a living if the economy forces them to significantly downsize their business. There may be that moment when you just decide "enough is enough" and it is time to move into the next phase of life. Even though the decision is made to sell, owners will not necessarily put their business on the market the next day. That is the time to start preparing the business for sale and start implementing the process for a successful sale of the business. **M&A**

CHAPTER 2
Positioning The Company For Sale

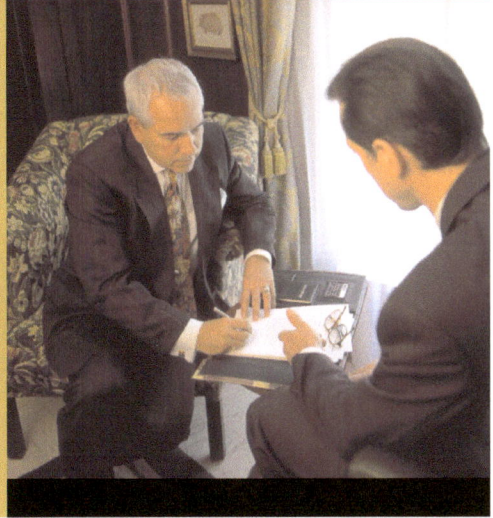

Planning ahead for a business sale can have tremendous benefits in terms of value and successfully closing the sale. There are many things in an ideal world that consultants would like business owners to do in order to properly position themselves for sale, but as a practical matter, businesses can't wave a magic wand and make all these things happen. For example, if you have one or two large customers, you can not automatically go out and find five or ten other customers to reduce your customer concentration. Yes, you can work on diversifying your customer base, but generally the assumption would be that you would be doing that anyway as part of your normal business operations.

There are, however, many things that you can do that will greatly enhance a business sale.

2.1 Maintain complete and accurate financial books and records. Two main benefits can be derived from having complete and accurate financial books and records. One benefit is that you have reliable information to guide you in your day-to-day business decisions, and the other is that you will have reliable information that a buyer can rely on when valuing your business. In order to have good books and records, you generally have to have a qualified individual that has the accounting expertise and knowledge necessary to capture and input the appropriate information and to provide output that is useful to the company. That person is the one who generally has to spend the most time in the sale process and is critical to the sale process. If that person has very limited knowledge and expertise, it usually makes the sale process much more difficult. This weakness is sometimes offset by

bringing in a part-time CFO or controller to assist in compiling and explaining all of the financial information required to sell the business.

2.2 Make full use of the accounting software used in the business.

Many businesses have robust accounting systems, but only use a fraction of the capabilities of those systems. In the sale process, buyers want to know a lot of detailed information including: (i) sales and profits by customers, (ii) sales and profits by product, (iii) sales and profits by departments or categories, (iv) vendor purchases and discounts, and (v) length of relationships with customers and vendors, etc. Many accounting programs are designed to allow businesses to easily capture that information, however, in order to do so, the appropriate information has to be input into the system on a regular and timely basis. Again, this information is extremely helpful both in making decisions in the ongoing operations of the business and in aiding a buyer in the analysis of your business.

2.3 Audited financial statements. During a booming economy and a booming M&A market, buyers and lenders are not nearly as discriminating in demanding audited financial statements. When the economy is not as robust, many sellers are not as healthy as they once may have been, and buyers and lenders are more discriminating. Audited financial statements become much more relevant in this environment. When financial statements are audited, the business has more credibility, not just in terms of the integrity of its numbers, but it also is a good reflection of management's desire to have a well-run company. Audited financials are also a significant help to buyers in obtaining financing from lenders who frequently require audited financial statements.

2.4 Maintain good governance, books and records. Many private companies do not have annual shareholder and board

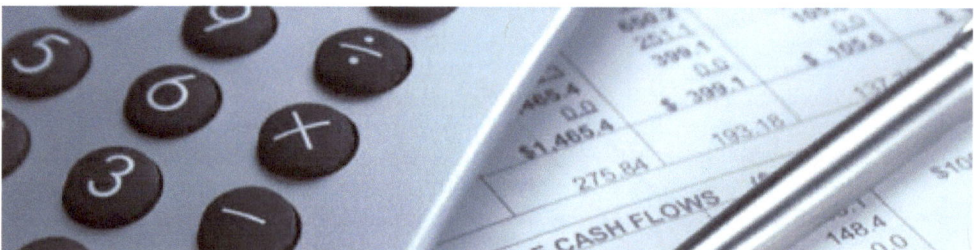

meeting minutes, do not properly track the issuance of their stock and do not maintain other books and records relating to the ongoing governance of their business. This is not a particularly egregious short-coming, but maintaining even minimal annual minutes and updating company books and records will be helpful in the sale of the business.

2.5   Maintain the facilities in a clean and attractive manner.

Buyers will want to visit your facilities. This is truly an instance where, "you only have one chance to make a good first impression." Clean and well-organized facilities will go a long way in enhancing the value of your business by lending credibility to the manner in which the business is run. The buyer does not have to worry about spending a lot of time and energy to bring the facilities up to their standards. This is also one of those tasks that has a two-fold benefit; (i) it will increase worker morale during the operation of the company; and (ii) enhances the value of the business in the sale

2.6   Maintain adequate management personnel. One of

the hardest things for many business owners is to give up the reins and allow others to manage various aspects of the business. This may work well while the business owner is around, but when you decide to sell and won't be around any longer, there will be a significant management gap. In order to position the company for sale, you should make every effort to develop good, strong management personnel in key positions that will allow for the uninterrupted growth and operation of the company. Management is a key issue that many buyers will look at. Private equity buyers (money funds) especially want to buy companies that have excellent management in place. This may not be as important to strategic buyers (buyers that are already in your industry or in related businesses), but may be important if they continue to operate the business on a stand-alone basis.

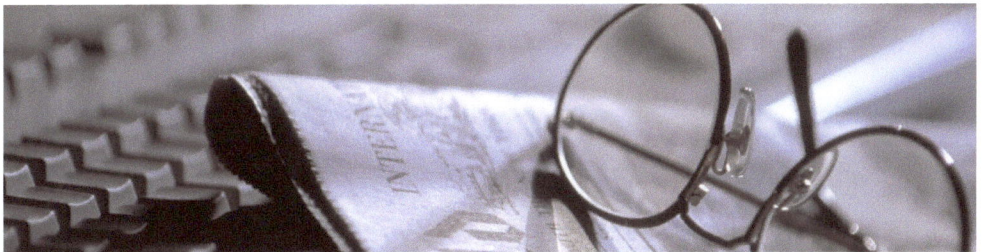

2.7 Continuing product development. Buyers buy the future and not the past. Ongoing research and development activity is required to make sure that your products and services stay relevant. Buyers want to see that the company can continue to grow at a reasonable pace. Buyers will project three to seven years down the road. They want to make sure that your products and services stay current during that period of time. Ongoing viable products and services are critical to Buyer's plans to either sell the company at a profit, or continue, if they elect to hold the company, to grow the company as part of their larger operation.

2.8 Investing and capital improvements. One of the first things buyers will assess is plant capacity or service capacity. Buying a company that has no capacity for growth may not present sufficient upside for buyers. Buyers would be faced with having to either move the facilities or make significant changes in order to obtain significant growth. Capacity can often times be dictated by the type of capital improvements that you make over time. If appropriate machines and tooling are upgraded as cash flow allows, the capacity of existing facilities may significantly increase the value of your business. In some cases, the need to make significant capital improvements may be what drives you to decide to sell the business. This is not necessarily a negative. If the business is poised for growth, but does not have the necessary capital, then this would be an ideal opportunity for an investor to purchase the company. This presents an opportunity to the buyer to make a modest investment that would substantially increase the company's sales and profitability. That upside should increase your sales price.

2.9 Customer diversification.
As I previously noted, this is certainly an area that is not easily controllable. Customer concentration is generally a negative in most buyer's eyes. Customer concentration can sometimes be overcome by having long-term agreements, however, long-term agreements are very rare except in the cases of government related projects. I will restate the obvious by noting that customer diversification is beneficial not only for ongoing operations, but in greatly improving the value of your business.

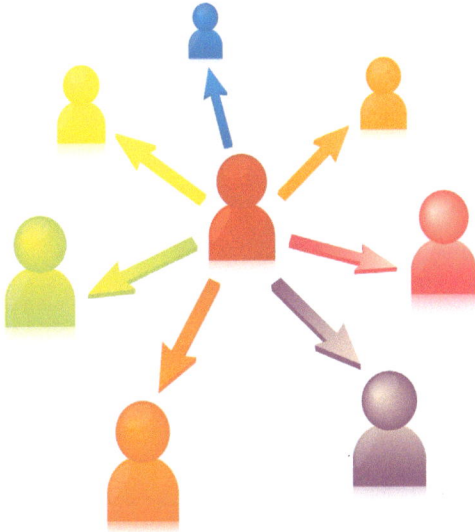

2.10 Alternative supply sources.

Determining who your suppliers are is often times more controllable than determining who your customers are. You should not become reliant on one or a limited number of suppliers. Whenever possible, alternative suppliers should be used or available so that buyers have the assurance that they can continue providing your products and services. **M&A**

CHAPTER 3
Sale Process Overview And Management

A well thought out sale process and management of that process throughout the transaction will yield a much higher sale value. In addition you greatly increase the chances of a successful closing. The M&A Law Firm manages the sales process from start to finish. A plan should be put in place that addresses:

(i)   the initial analysis of the business;

(ii)   preparation of appropriate seller diligence;

(iii)   identification of the appropriate investment banker to represent you in the sale;

(iv)   setting up and populating a data room with all relevant documents relating to seller's business;

(v)   oversight of the preparation of the offering memorandum;

(vi)   coordination of the marketing effort to contact all appropriate buyers, obtain indications of interest, set up management meetings and finalize letters of intent;

(vii)   complete all negotiations and documentation for final closing of the transaction.

The foregoing process is achieved through the M&A Law Firm's oversight and working with other consultants including, but not limited to, accountants, financial consultants, investment bankers, estate planners, other legal specialists and various technical consultants. M&A

CHAPTER 4
Creating Value Through Preparation And Analysis

4.1   Prepare initial business profile. In order to effectively begin communicating with the various advisors that will be required in the sale of your business, it is very helpful to prepare an initial business profile. The M&A Law Firm will ask for some basic information and, using that information, will prepare a summary business profile that is generally two to three pages long and gives a thumb nail sketch of your business. This information is usually information that is not available on your website or in your general marketing materials. This initial business profile, along with your other web information and marketing information and limited financial information, will be used as the basic starting point in explaining your business to your other advisors.

4.2 Seller diligence. The type of information that buyers will want to know is generally not a mystery. The questions that buyers ask on their due diligence list and the type of information that they request is fairly consistent from buyer to buyer. The M&A Law Firm takes a proactive approach and engages in "seller diligence" at the front end of the transaction to answer those questions.

A seller diligence report should be prepared at the outset of the transaction. The M&A Law Firm has determined what groups or individuals are best suited to provide this service and will assist the seller in selecting the transaction consultants that are best suited to perform your seller diligence. A seller diligence report will include financial results with appropriate adjustments to determine actual profit, and general descriptive information about your business including facilities, employees, history, product description, competition, environmental matters, working capital analysis, sales and profit analysis by customer and by product or services, and a quality of earnings analysis which assesses the accuracy of each of the income statement and balance sheet accounts.

This seller diligence report provides you with several significant advantages which include: (i) discovering issues or potential problems that you can correct prior to presenting the business to a buyer; (ii) giving you far greater insight into your business than you may have had using your standard accounting and reporting methods; (iii) identifying all add backs that increase profits which will increase sales value; (iv) giving buyers the information they need before they ask for it; and (v) substantially eliminating the problem of buyers renegotiating terms and conditions after the execution of an LOI based on discoveries by buyer in their own due diligence.

The seller diligence report can literally be "worth its weight in gold." The identification of additional add-backs, analysis of appropriate working capital to be transferred to buyer and the ability to address any issues and present the business in the most positive light will all lead to increased value.

4.3 Creation of seller data room.

In a typical transaction, a buyer, following signing of a letter of intent, will present a lengthy list of questions to be answered and documents to be provided by seller as part of buyer's due diligence. As part of the proactive seller diligence process noted above, the M&A Law Firm will set up a data room at the outset of the transaction. The data room is a virtual storage room for all the documentation in a typical transaction. The data room is a secure site managed by the M&A Law Firm. In the course of putting together the seller diligence report, the M&A Law Firm will work with you and the investment banker to populate the data room with all of your documentation that a buyer would normally require. This documentation will include items such as, articles, bylaws, minutes, stock certificates, financial statements, tax returns, employment handbooks and information, insurance contracts, lender agreements, leases, contracts with customers and suppliers, employment agreements, etc.

It is much easier for sellers to obtain and copy information for the data room during the seller diligence process than it is to try to do all of this work following the signing of the letter of intent. Note that the documents only need to be copied one time since they will be in the data room and the M&A Law Firm can control who has access to those documents. The preparation of a seller diligence report along with putting documents in the data room will result in attracting a larger number of qualified buyers and greatly increasing the chances of a quick and successful closing. **M&A**

CHAPTER 5
Valuing The Business

5.1   Factors affecting value.

The first thing business sellers want to know is what value they can expect to receive for their company. The "real answer" is that valuation is dependent upon many things including, but not limited to: (i) company size; (ii) industry; (iii) customer diversification; (iv) profitability; (v) growth potential, (vi) technology; (vii) management; (viii) capacity, etc. Furthermore, value truly can be "in the eyes of the beholder." As noted below, the key is finding that buyer who sees the greatest value in your business. Your investment banker can give you some good insight into what your business may be worth in the market place.

5.2   How value is determined.

The objective is to find a buyer that has a unique need for a particular seller that will cause that buyer to pay a premium. Values are expressed in terms of a multiple of EBITDA (earnings before interest, taxes, depreciation and amortization). Buyers of a middle market business typically want a return on their investment in the range of fifteen to twenty five percent. Based on that return, a buyer would pay in the range of 4 to 7 times EBITDA. Service companies may be valued more on multiples of revenues (one times revenue as a base line). Companies come in all shapes and sizes and every company has unique features that will lead to its own unique valuation.

5.3   Getting the right valuation.
Gathering information from friends, other business acquaintances, cocktail parties and general news items can be very misleading. Sellers will oftentimes focus on

certain multiples that are reported for a transaction. Those reports or statistics, however, do not contain many of the underlying details that are relevant in assessing actual values such as the amount of profit actually reported, potential growth of seller and synergies between buyer and seller. Sellers should not obtain a formal appraisal, but should consult with the M&A Law Firm and their investment banker to assess the potential value of their company.

5.4 Purchase price does not include asset value. A common misconception is that a buyer will pay the value as determined by an EBITDA multiple plus the value of seller's assets. Seller asset value is not added to the purchase price. In return for the purchase price, the buyer expects to get a business that has all of the necessary assets to generate the EBITDA that was used to calculate the purchase price. If the value of the underlying assets was added to the purchase price, the buyer would be paying twice for the business. You should, however, be paid for any "excess working capital" that is on hand at closing. **M&A**

CHAPTER 6
Selecting The Investment Banker

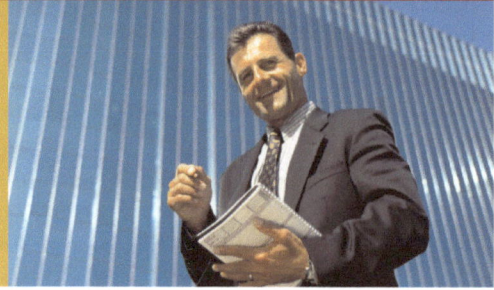

The selection of your investment banker is the most important step that you will take in the sale of your business. The investment banker becomes the face of your transaction and is the party responsible for obtaining the best and highest offer for your company.

6.1   Initial investment banker search. As much care should be taken in selecting your investment banker as you would take in selecting the appropriate doctor for a specific medical procedure. Although you would not hire a foot surgeon to do your brain surgeon, many business owners hire investment bankers that are not well suited to represent their business. The M&A Law Firm conducts a nationwide search (in some cases a worldwide search) for the appropriate investment banker to represent your business. The purpose of this search is to identify at least three, but not more than five, investment bankers that would be extremely well-suited to represent your business. These selected investment bankers would be invited to interviews which would last approximately 1 1/2 hours each for the purpose of determining which investment banker is the most qualified to represent you in the sale of your business.

6.2   Investment banker interviews. In order to make the investment banker interviews meaningful, it will be necessary to provide the investment banker with as much information about your company as possible. Generally, the seller diligence report should be completed, or substantially completed, before the investment banker interviews. This will allow the investment bankers to obtain a complete picture of your business. They can then use that information to prepare their "pitch book" which is a compilation of information that they will provide to you setting forth their expertise, the manner in which they will market your company, potential buyers of your company and what they believe will be the value of your company in the market place. Investment bankers do not charge for the time and effort to prepare this information or in attending the interviews. This is a time and opportunity that you can use to obtain extremely good insights into how these professionals value your company in the real world M&A market.

6.3　Key investment banker characteristics. As part of the interview process, the M&A Law Firm has prepared a 40 point questionnaire for use in determining who would be the best investment banker for your company. The assumption is that any of the investment bankers invited to interview would be excellent representatives. The interview process provides you with the opportunity to select that investment banker that best fits your needs and that you feel most comfortable working with. The following are some of the primary considerations to be addressed in determining which investment banker to use: (i) industry specialty and experience; (ii) the size of transactions handled by the investment banker; (iii) personnel assigned by investment banker to this transaction; (iv) method of investment banker compensation; (v) overall quality of materials and presentation; (vi) reputation/referrals; and (vii) what, if any, "red flags" come up during the interview.

6.4　Key investment banker agreement terms. Once the investment banker has been selected, the M&A Law Firm will review the investment banker agreement to make sure that the investment banker incentives are properly aligned with your goals.

6.4.1 Key man provision. A provision should be included that requires specific personnel of the investment banker to work on your transaction. In the event one or more of those personnel are no longer with the investment banking firm, or cannot perform their services for any reason, provisions would be included to allow you to either terminate or modify the agreement at your discretion.

6.4.2 Compensation criteria. Clear terms and conditions should be set forth regarding how the investment banker will be compensated. This will include addressing what is included in determining total value of your company and the timing of payments made to the investment banker (generally payments to the investment banker should be made when you receive your proceeds).

6.4.3 Retainer v. success fee. Most investment bankers will require some form and amount of monthly retainer. That retainer, however, should be minimal compared to the success fee which would be paid upon conclusion of the transaction.

6.4.4 Structuring the success fee. The success fee should be structured in a manner that will incentivize the investment banker to both give your transaction its full and complete attention and obtain the highest value possible.

6.4.5 Termination. Investment banking agreements generally have what is referred to as a "tail." The tail is the period of time following the actual termination of the agreement when the investment banker would still be entitled to a commission if there is a sale to a buyer that was identified prior to the actual termination. Generally, this tail period should not exceed twelve months and it should be limited to those buyers who have actually signed confidentiality agreements and have requested detailed information about your company. **M&A**

CHAPTER 7
The Marketing Process

After the investment banker is selected, the investment banker will begin the preparation of the marketing materials for use in the marketing of your company.

7.1   Preparation of confidential offering memorandum.

Using the information that you have already put together as part of the seller diligence process, including the seller diligence report, data room and other general information, the investment banker will prepare a confidential offering memorandum ("COM"). The COM will reflect some of the same information provided in the seller diligence report but will, in general, be a much more marketing oriented report and will contain much greater detail regarding the company's products, operations, customers and vendors, and other relevant information.

7.2   Preparation of buyer list.
The investment banker is charged with the task of identifying potential buyers for your company. In some cases this may result in a list of two or three hundred potential buyers, and in other cases, in more targeted offerings, may only involve 20 or 30 potential buyers. You will always have the final authority on which buyers the investment banker will contact. You may not want to contact certain potential buyers in order to avoid disclosure to customers or existing competitors.

7.3   Teaser letters.
The first step in contacting potential buyers will be to send out teaser letters. These teaser letters will have limited information so that potential buyers are not able to specifically identify your company, but will have sufficient

information to bring an opportunity to the attention of prospective buyers.

7.4 Signing of Non-disclosure agreements and receipt of confidential offering memorandums.

Those buyers receiving teaser letters that express an interest in getting further information will then be sent a non-disclosure agreement (the "NDA"). The NDA requires that potential buyers keep any seller information sent to them in strictest confidence. When the investment banker receives the signed NDA back from the buyer, a confidential offering memorandum will then be sent to those buyers.

7.5 Telephone follow-up.

If the investment banker has not received a response from its teaser letter, then the investment banker will follow-up with a phone call or numerous phone calls to make sure that those buyers are aware of the transaction. This process oftentimes results in additional interest by buyers who may have overlooked the teaser letter or needed some additional prodding in order to become more involved in the process.

7.6 Solicitation of letters of intent (or indication of interest).

Those perspective buyers who have received the confidential offering memorandum will be asked to provide indications of interest or letters of intent (terms that may be used interchangeably), on or before a date certain. After receiving these initial letters and after some further negotiations between the investment banker and prospective buyers, you then select, with the input of your advisors, those prospective buyers that you would like to provide with additional information through the management presentation process. **M&A**

CHAPTER 8
Management Presentations

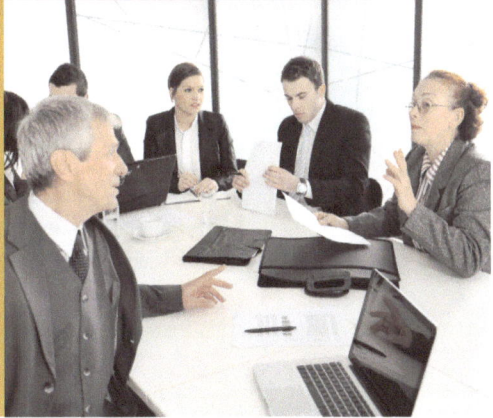

Management presentations consist of inviting a prospective buyer to your facilities (meetings may also be held offsite) to obtain additional information. Various key company personnel will present detailed information regarding your company and give buyers the opportunity to ask questions. Each presentation, along with the question and answer session, will generally take about three hours. Buyers will also generally want to take a tour of your facilities while they are in the area.

The number of management presentations will vary depending upon how many "serious" offers are received. Five presentations is usually an ideal number, however, there may be more or less presentations based on buyer interest. **M&A**

www.MandAlawyer.com   21

CHAPTER 9
Buyer Selection And Execution Of Letter Of Intent

The prospective buyers who attended the management presentations may submit additional follow up questions to help them in preparing their final Letters of Intent (LOI). Negotiations are at their peak starting with the receipt of these final LOIs (which really are not final until the negotiations are complete). The investment banker will have significant communication with these buyers during this short period of time (generally one to three weeks) in order to encourage buyers to provide better pricing and terms if they want to be the winning bidder. This is also a time period in which a knowledgeable and experienced attorney can add a tremendous amount of value in working with you and the investment banker to come up with the best structure and means to maximize value depending on each buyer's needs. After the "last ounce of negotiations" is completed, a LOI is signed with the chosen buyer.

The prospective buyers that were invited to attend the management presentations will have access to the seller diligence report before they submit their final letters of intent. Buyers will then have a complete picture of the business they are trying to buy and should not expect any surprises in their own due diligence. Since these buyers have substantially all of the information that they need to evaluate your company, they are much less likely to try to renegotiate terms later in the sale process. Buyer should not find anything in its due diligence that has not already been uncovered and presented as part of your seller diligence report.

The availability of the seller diligence report, provides you with a much higher comfort level that terms won't be renegotiated, that the transaction will get closed, and that the closing will occur in a shorter period of time. **M&A**

CHAPTER 10

Review And Analysis Of Letters Of Intent

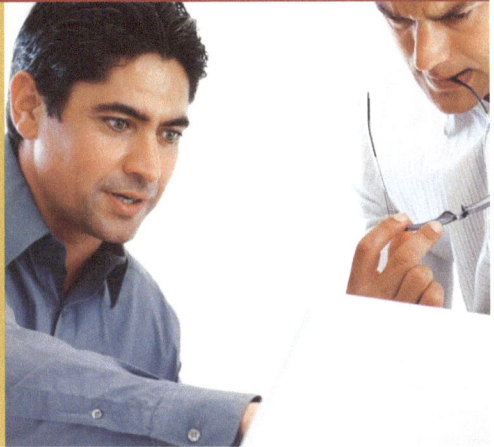

A well drafted, detailed letter of intent is a very important part of a successful transaction.

10.1 Comparison of letters of intent. The M&A Law Firm has developed a template that sets forth all of the key issues that should be included as part of a letter of intent. In addition to identifying the issues, the template also has a column titled "seller guidelines." The seller guidelines column will contain terms and conditions for various key points that buyer is expected to meet in order to remain competitive in the bidding process. The third column of the template provides the space for buyers to put in their specific proposed terms and conditions. Each buyer will be asked to complete the template. By going through this process, you receive letters of intent from buyers that address all of the key issues which allows you to compare offers on an "apples-to-apples" basis to see which offer is truly the best offer.

10.2 Review and analysis of letters of intent. The attorney and investment banker will lead the charge with your input to negotiate with prospective buyers to obtain the best terms and conditions possible in the letter of intent.

10.3 Qualification of buyers.

One of the key roles that the investment banker should play in the sale process is the qualification of potential buyers. Getting a letter of intent with excellent terms and conditions is meaningless if the buyer is not able to complete the transaction. It is important for the investment banker to assess the ability of the buyer to complete the transaction and for you to understand the various strengths and weaknesses of potential buyers.

10.4 Key letter of intent points.

It is important that all key terms and conditions be included in the letter of intent. Failure to include certain key provisions will only result in difficulty, delay and possible failure of the transaction at a later point. Some investment bankers prefer to have their seller clients sign vague letters of intent to get buyers "hooked." That hook, however, usually ends up getting stuck in the seller.

The following key terms and conditions should be addressed in the letter of intent:

    (i)   structure of the transaction:

          (a)   asset purchase
          (b)   stock purchase
          (c)   seller retention of part of the company

    (ii)   price and terms of payment (earnout conditions)

    (iii)   escrow holdback terms and conditions

    (iv)   allocation of purchase price (determines ordinary v. capital gain)

    (v)   working capital target

    (vi)   security for any deferred payments

    (vii)   lease or purchase of seller real property

    (viii) indemnity limitations and "deductibles"

    (ix)   noncompetition provisions

    (x)   sales tax liability

    (xi)   timing (exclusivity = how long is seller expected to stay off the market)

    (xii)   financing contingencies, if any

    (xiii) limiting contact with customers, suppliers and employees

    (xiv) compensation for continued employment

    (xv)   nonbinding nature of the letter of intent

M&A

CHAPTER 11
Due Diligence

Due diligence is generally referred to as the buyer's investigation of your business. This is the part of the process that sellers generally fear most. But if seller diligence has been performed there should be no reason to fear buyer due diligence. Almost all of your work in meeting buyer's due diligence requirements will have been completed as part of the seller diligence process.

Seller diligence allows information to be immediately available to buyer prior to the signing of the letter of intent instead of waiting 30 to 60 days for buyer diligence to produce that information.

11.1 Buyer diligence list. Buyers will generally provide you with three different lists from; (i) buyer; (ii) buyer's accountants; and (iii) buyer's legal counsel. The information already available in the data room and in the seller diligence report will generally result in addressing 90-95% of the information and document requests in those lists.

11.2 Buyer diligence schedule. Buyer may want to have various consultants and personnel visit your company and perform various due diligence tasks. Buyer should, at the outset of the diligence process, provide you with a detailed schedule showing which parties will be conducting certain portions of the diligence and on what dates they would need to meet with your personnel. Certain personnel may be "off limits" to protect your confidentiality.

11.3 Financing. One of the biggest benefits to performing seller diligence, is that the buyer can provide its lender, on day one, with the seller diligence report along with access to the data room. The seller diligence report and data room will provide the lender with substantially all of the information that it needs in order to assess its ability to provide the financing that the buyer may need to complete the transaction. If the seller diligence report and the data room are not completed, the lender or lenders would have to wait until buyer completes its due diligence and then start the process of determining its ability to finance the transaction. This can substantially slow down a transaction and many times may derail a transaction. **M&A**

CHAPTER 12
Preparation Of Legal Documents

12.1 Purchase Agreement
12.2 Schedules to the purchase agreement
12.3 Ancillary documents

12.1 Preparation of Purchase Agreement. The LOI is the road map that is used to prepare the purchase agreement. If the LOI is not sufficiently detailed the process of drafting, negotiating and completing the purchase agreement will be much more difficult. You should demand that the buyer provide you with a first draft of the purchase agreement within two to three weeks following the signing of the LOI. This then allows you to look at any remaining issues that may need to be resolved, start the preparation of the schedules that are part of the purchase agreement, and have a better road map to closing.

The availability of the seller diligence report and a fully populated data room will also allow buyer's counsel to begin drafting purchase agreements immediately following the execution of the letter of intent. This can accelerate the closing by several weeks.

12.2 Preparation of schedules to the purchase agreement. Preparation of schedules is usually one of the steps that delays a closing. Schedules to the purchase agreement are prepared by seller. The schedules are "lists" and not generally "documents." Schedules will include lists of items such as, liens, bank accounts, contracts, assets, receivables, consents required to transfer contracts, employees, insurance policies, stock ownership, leases, etc. Much of the information to be included on the schedules can be obtained from a review of the documents in the data room, however, there will be other information that will have to be obtained independently by seller. Your investment banker and your legal counsel will work closely with you in the preparation of the schedules.

12.3 Preparation of ancillary documents.

Other documents prepared as part of the sale process may include;

(i)	promissory note
(ii)	security agreement
(iii)	leases or real property purchase agreements
(iv)	employment agreements
(v)	releases
(vi)	resolutions of buyer and seller
(vii)	restrictive covenant agreements
(viii)	assignment and assumption of liabilities agreement

M&A

CHAPTER 13

Taxation

13.1 Asset Sale

13.2 Stock Sale

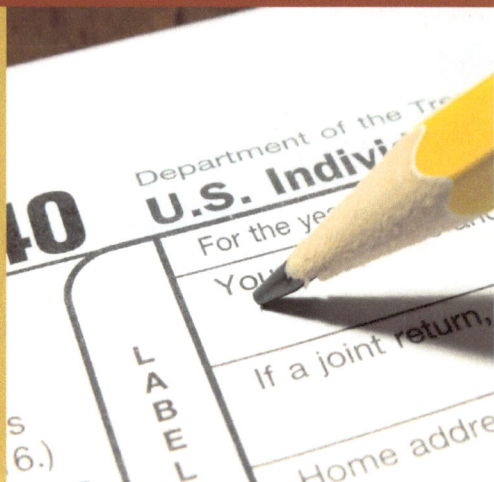

13.1 Asset Sale. The best way to understand an asset sale is to view the selling entity as a "box" and all of seller's assets and liabilities are in the box. Those assets include receivables, equipment, inventory, software, company names and other intangibles (phone numbers, web domains, etc.) the "box" also contains company liabilities such as accounts payable, bank obligations and other operating liabilities. In an asset sale the buyer looks in the box and takes out specifically identified assets and assumes specifically identified liabilities. Those assets and liabilities are removed from the "box" and put into buyer's entity. The assets and liabilities are replaced by cash, cash equivalents and maybe some deferred purchase price documents such as notes. You still own the box (or the company in this case) and will probably distribute the consideration out of the company to the shareholders after the transaction is closed.

A common misconception is that the company cannot transfer its name and other intangibles in an asset sale since the buyer is not acquiring the selling entity. That is not correct. The goodwill and other intangibles are treated as assets just like inventory and equipment and can be transferred as part of the asset sale.

Many buyers prefer the asset sale structure over a stock purchase. In a stock sale the buyer gets everything in the "box" whether they want it or not because they become the owners of the box. This usually brings up a concern on buyer's part that there may be liabilities in the box that it is not aware of (or are not capable of being identified) at the time of closing.

13.1.1 "C" corporation asset sale.

A "C" corporation asset sale is taxable on gain at the corporate level and the shareholders are taxed again when that gain is distributed to them (commonly referred to as a double tax). An asset sale of a "C" corporation could result in additional taxes of 25% or more depending on the state in which you are located. Clearly, an asset sale of a "C" corporation is not a preferred structure.

13.1.2 "S" corporation (or LLC) asset sale.

"S" corporations and LLCs are "pass through entities" so there is no double tax (except for "S" corporation state tax, if any). The owners are taxed one time on the sale proceeds.

13.1.3 Determination of tax in an asset sale.

When the assets are sold, the purchase price is equal to the consideration paid for the assets plus the amount of liabilities assumed by the buyer. This total is then allocated to the specific assets acquired. For example, if the sale price is $50M ($40M cash equivalent and $10M assumed liabilities) the allocation may be as follows:

Receivables	$4M	(actual book balance)
Equipment	$3M	(depreciated tax basis)
Inventory	$5M	(actual book/tax balance)
Other current assets	$1M	(actual book/tax balance)
Covenant not to compet	$1M	(negotiated amount for noncompete)
Goodwill	$36M	(balance of purchase price)

Based on the foregoing allocation, seller would have capital gain of $36M (goodwill allocation) and ordinary income of $1M (the allocation to the covenant not to compete). No gain would be recognized on the other assets if they are sold at their tax basis. Additional ordinary income, however, would be incurred to the extent that there is an

allocation of the purchase price to equipment, inventory, or other assets that exceeds their tax basis. Such additional allocations should be avoided by sellers if possible. Also note that sales tax may be due and payable on the value of the equipment being transferred.

13.1.4 Cash free and debt free sale. Sales are generally structured on a "cash free" and "debt free" basis. This means that seller will keep all of its cash, but will also have to pay off all of its interest bearing debt (typically its working capital line of credit and equipment loans). As a result, cash is not included as part of the purchase price and is not included in the allocation schedule.

13.2 Stock sale. When you sell your stock, the excess of the amount paid for the stock over your basis in the stock will be taxed as a capital gain. Stock sales are clearly favored by owners of "C" corporations. In the case of "S" corporations and LLCs, the difference in an asset sale and stock sale are not material to the overall transaction so those owners have more flexibility. Don't forget, however, that in an asset sale there may be a state corporate tax plus sales tax on the equipment. **M&A**

CHAPTER 14
Document Signing And Closing

Most transactions are structured as a "sign and close." This means that the purchase agreement and the ancillary documents are signed on the same day that the closing occurs. As a practical matter, by the time buyer completes any additional due diligence and all the legal documents are prepared, reviewed, revised and finalized and all other parts of the transactions have been completed, the parties are generally ready to close.

There are rare transactions, however, where the parties will execute a purchase agreement ahead of the closing. In those cases, the purchase agreement will contain certain closing conditions that have to be met in the interim period between signing and closing. Those conditions may include obtaining certain customer or leasehold consents and obtaining financing. As noted, this type of "sign and delayed close" are the exception and not the rule. M&A

CHAPTER 15
The Closing

15.1 The Closing. The closing, with the advent of the internet, has become somewhat anti-climatic except for the thrill of the acceptance of the sale proceeds. Generally, closings are "virtual." The parties do not come together in a room to sign documents and exchange consideration. During the last week to ten days of a transaction, the attorneys are typically finalizing documents and obtaining signatures of the parties on those documents. The signed documents are then held in trust by the attorneys with the understanding that the signatures are to be effective as of the closing date and the documents can be delivered as of the closing date. When the closing date arrives, all the signed documents should have been properly executed and deposited with the appropriate attorney and all that is left to complete the transaction is the wiring of the funds. The funds are wired on the closing date, you acknowledge receipt of the funds and the transaction is closed. **M&A**

15.2 The Closing Celebration. Following the closing, the investment banker may take this opportunity to bring various parties together for a closing dinner or other event to celebrate the completion of the transaction. This event will often times be dependent upon the availability and location of the parties. A celebration will certainly be in order if you have engaged in and completed a well run sales process. **M&A**

Conclusion

Selling your business is an important life event and can have a major impact on your finances, family and lifestyle. The M&A Law Firm is here to guide you through all aspects of the sale process. Experienced and highly trained counsel will make sure that the process is conducted in a manner that provides the best opportunity to complete your transaction on the most favorable terms.

For questions and further assistance in the sale of your business, contact the M&A Law Firm at:

THE M&A LAW FIRM
Roger L. Neu, J.D., CPA
2040 Main Street, Suite 710
Irvine, California
(949) 863-1700

EMAIL: rneuoffice@aol.com
WEB: www.MandAlawyer.com

This document is only intended to be an overview of the business sale process and should not be relied upon specifically as providing legal advice. **M&A**

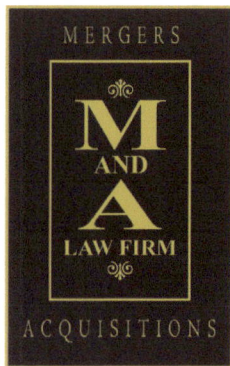

MERGERS

M
AND
A
LAW FIRM

ACQUISITIONS

www.ingramcontent.com/pod-product-compliance
Lightning Source LLC
Chambersburg PA
CBHW041718200326

41520CB00001B/152